Water: Save a Lot with Our Recycle Robot

By:

Christopher Jackson, Kylie Mitchell,
Mateo Clemons and Naomi Wintz

FIRST JrFLL Team Koo Koo Birds – Raleigh, NC

With Mentors Samantha Shefte and Garret Dixon

Forward By: The Honorable Ambassador Andrew Young

Afterward By: Louis Martin-Vega, PhD
Dean of the College of Engineering
North Carolina State of University

Supported as an Educational Partner by:
Secretary Michael Regan, NC Department of Water Quality

NC
Environmental
Quality

Forward:

Supporting YOUNG Global Leaders who Care for Tomorrow... Today!

As the best friend of Martin Luther King, Jr., I learned as a very young collegiate that the struggles of African Americans over the ages was a reflection of inequality and injustice that existed all over the world in many different forms for centuries. One of the most successful strategies of the Civil Rights Movement was to make our dreams for a better America, the dreams of a better world. Our American struggle for freedom and equality was and is the struggle of every man, woman, boy or girl globally who dare to DREAM BIG and make the world a better place. Dreaming Big and Acting Better to make the world a better place- is exactly what Christopher, Kylie, Mateo and Naomi have done in this book, Water: Save a lot with Our Recycle Root.

I am grateful at 85 years YOUNG to be an icon with these Elementary authors – ages 6 and 7. Having travelled around the world as a US Congressman, Mayor of Atlanta, and as the first African American US Ambassador to the United Nations, I know how devastating the lack of water, especially clean water can be to children, families and to nations. Congratulations to this For Inspiration and Recognition of Science and Technology (FIRST) Lego League Junior Team for taking their year-long training about water to heart and to a higher level where they could share this message of using science and technology to conserve water through this very clever book and offering it to the United Nations to help other young children worldwide learn about Saving Water- to give prominence to World Water Day on March 22, 2018. The Science and Technology vision that these young kids express in this book is a great example of children who care for others around the world to demonstrate true global citizenship and leadership through knowledge, education and action. I am proud to be a part of their global water conservation awareness by their inclusion of my vision of Aquaponics water recycles system, which I believe can feed 20 million by 2020. I am honored to be forever a member of this FIRST Jr. FLL team in spirit and in support.

It is comforting to know that there are future leaders like Christopher, Kylie, Mateo and Naomi who are already thinking about how we all can protect our planet to save the world as we know it today for tomorrow and beyond...   This children's book not only raises awareness through education of water conservation, but it also embodies the Aqua Adventure theme of the 2018 FIRST Competition and challenges other young readers to think scientifically and technologically about new water conservation ideas and to be global citizens and philanthropists by saving water to give water to those in need. Global STEM leaders who continue to Think Young will Impact our world to be better- with our continued nurturing and support. Thanks Team Koo Koo Birds for making Saving Water everywhere as the way in which we should show we care and a way to continue Our Movement that Civil Rights are Human Rights for a better world everywhere.

Best Wishes for a Great Future that will allow your lives to continue to be Impactful to Others. I support you and the world needs you too.

The Honorable Ambassador Andrew Young

We dedicate this book to Our Parents who continue

to give us unconditional love and support

And to

Dr. Louise Tarver Jackson,

Mother, Grandmother, and Elementary Educator

who has given a living legacy to encourage all

children to Enjoy Learning through Exploration

and with the Kindness to Help Others.

Water, Water Everywhere
We save water because we care.

It's in the ground, it's in the air,
But clean fresh water is becoming rare.

We drink water for our health
It's a part of how we care for ourselves.
We love the beach and ocean clear
Because water waves and land meet there.

In the summertime, we love the pool
Splashing water keeps us cool.

Every day we use soap and water
To bathe and wash our bodies proper.

Clean fresh water is a good drink
We try not to waste it in the sink.
When we brush our teeth we turn off the faucet,
To save water and stop the loss of it.

We wish the world had enough water for all;
If only we could save rainfall.

Saving water, saving plants and animals is what it's all about
We would be protecting our entire climate from
Hurricaines or Drought.

It's a balance you see between water, the earth and the particles in our air,

They affect our climate, from cold or hot or cloudy to fair

that's why we care!

See we all need to protect the environment with water to continue to thrive

Without it life on Earth for plants,animals,fish and people can not survive.

So save water to show you care
Everyone needs more clean water... everywhere.

Lakes, rivers, ponds, and streams,
I have a dream that they are all clean.

From Flint to Puerto Rico or Ghana's Coast
There are some cities and countries around the world that need clean water the most.

So many things that we can change,
To save water if we use our brains.

Get only what you need to use,
To wash your body,clothes, and shoes

To make your meals and take a drink
Don't waste a drop is what we think !
We must be wise in how we use it
Find a smart new way and always choose it.

What if we made a Water Robot ?
A Robot that Recycles Water a lot.
A Robot that Recycles Water is that Aquaponics ?
Where sea life grows food ... honest ?

Aquaponics not only helps the fish
It can also grow food for a tasty dish.

We are talking a water robot with plants, fish and even worms

Aquaponics can help feed the world in many forms.

It's Ambassador Young's vision to meet all peoples' needs,
With Aquaponics-20 million by 2020 is what we can feed.

Imagine all the food we could share,

If people used Aquaponics everywhere !

The cycle of life is about caring you see
One takes care of the other   just like you and me.
See saving water helps us all, To stay healthy and stand tall.

Our climate cycles water to rise with Evaporation.
Then water droplets get together to form Condensation.
Condensation will expand to produce Cloud Formation.
And Clouds release rain for our much needed Precipitation.

Saving our water is called Con-ser-vation.

Conserving water can save all nations.

So tell your friends, family and loved ones with you,
In this age, clean water should be for all, not just a few.

Water may be everywhere
But we could use it up we fear.

So let's all help out saving water to do our share,

To show the world that we really care.

The End

Afterward:

"Providing Access to Clean Water" has been identified by the National Academy of Engineering as one the 14 Grand Challenges for Engineering in the 21st Century. As pointed out by the young authors of this lovely book, the motivation for this being such a Grand Challenge is clear…. the availability of clean water for drinking, sanitation and other uses is a critical problem not only in Flint, Puerto Rico and Ghana's coast but in many cities and countries around the world.

Not only do the young authors understand this problem, they also propose creative approaches to solving the problem. Their "Water Recycle Robot" and related ideas that they describe so well in this book are both intriguing and innovative and reflect their awareness of the important role that technology can play in addressing this Grand Challenge. Engineers strive every day to convert ideas into reality to solve global societal problems and this is exactly what these "future engineers" and their book set out to accomplish.

Unfortunately, even today in 2018 about 1 out of every 6 people living still do not have access to water. In some countries half the population still do not have access to safe drinking water. Many students and faculty at engineering colleges, such as ours at North Carolina State University, are now focusing more of their work on this worldwide human challenge. But we still need more to join us in this effort.

On behalf of our engineering community, I would like to congratulate Christopher, Kylie, Mateo and Naomi for writing this outstanding book. You have demonstrated that even at a very early age it is possible to understand and propose creative solutions to a global problem of this nature. Thank you for doing this and it is our hope that your work will inspire many others to, in your own words, "save water to do our share and show the world that we care".

Louis A. Martin-Vega, PhD

Dean, College of Engineering

NC State University

Raleigh, NC

<h1 style="text-align:center"><u>DIY Aquaponics System</u></h1>

Here's what you (and an adult) will need:
- 2 Liter-Bottle
- 1 Net Cup
- 1 Dremel Tool
- Peat Pellet with Manoa Lettuce Starter
- Chopstick
- A guppy fish

Step by Step:

Step 1. Cut the top off the clear bottle (make sure the label is removed, you'll need the bottle clear so the sunlight can get through).

Step 2. Turn it upside down and cut out a hole for the net cup.

Step 3. Insert net cup with peat pellet and Manoa Lettuce Starter.

Step 4. Drill air holes into the bottle for fish and chopstick to hold the top of the bottle into the bottom.

Step 5. Fill water into bottom of bottle and put fish inside. Make sure to set out the water in a shallow pan for 24 hours (1 day) so the chlorine in the will evaporate.

Step 6. Put the top into the bottom bottle upside down and put net cup in with peat pellet and Manoa Lettuce.

Step 7. Place in a sunny spot where sunlight can get through the clear plastic to do its work. Sunlight will keep the "cycle" in motion. Guppies live quite happily by eating the plants and algae that grow in the bottle, keeping the system in balance.

Glossary

Aquaponics – Creating a mini-world full of plants and animals

Climate – The different weather in an area of land

Condensation - When water goes from a gas to a liquid and forms into water droplets

Conservation – The saving of something

Drought – The lack of water

Evaporation - When water vapor is brought from the ground to the clouds

Healthy – Good to use

Hurricanes – Strong turning winds and water that can damage buildings and harm people, can cause strong flooding

Particles – Small things that float around in the air

Precipitation - The falling down of water from the clouds

Protect – Saving something from harm

Rare – Not a lot of something, hard to come by

Recycle - To save and reuse